International Conference on Information Systems and Management Science (ISMS 2018)

Misida, Malta
22 – 23 February 2018

ISBN: 978-1-5108-5880-0

Printed from e-media with permission by:

Curran Associates, Inc.
57 Morehouse Lane
Red Hook, NY 12571

Some format issues inherent in the e-media version may also appear in this print version.

Printed by Curran Associates, Inc. (2018)

For permission requests, please contact International Association of Academicians Connecting Scholars, Scientists and Engineers (IAASSE) at the address below.

International Association of Academicians Connecting Scholars, Scientists and Engineers (IAASSE)

www.iaasse.org
info@iaasse.org

Additional copies of this publication are available from:

Curran Associates, Inc.
57 Morehouse Lane
Red Hook, NY 12571 USA
Phone: 845-758-0400
Fax: 845-758-2633
Email: curran@proceedings.com
Web: www.proceedings.com

TABLE OF CONTENTS

1

AGILE PROJECT MANAGEMENT IN UNIVERSITY-INDUSTRY COLLABORATION PROJECTS

Marika Säisä, Katariina Tiura & Rita Matikainen
ICT Unit, Faculty of Business, ICT and Chemical Engineering,
Turku University of Applied Sciences

ABSTRACT

Main goal of a project is to complete the project in agreed time within the allocated budget and desired quality standards. Yet, especially in big IT projects a failure of one or more of the factors is rather a rule than an exception. Agile project management has been a rising trend for several years as an IT project management method. The aim of the agile project management is to reduce the failures in projects by concentrating on delivering the most valued parts of the project and making agile changes to the project if needed. Several IT-companies use different agile project management ways to manage the project. Scrum is one of most used ones. In Engineering Education, students ought to gain competences relevant for the requirements of the working life. Thus, students not only have to master a deep working knowledge of technical fundamentals, but also project management skills. This case study presents how Scrum project management skills can be integrated into university-industry collaboration projects. This study focuses on "the FIRMA" that is a learning environment of the ICT Education and Research Unit of Turku University of Applied Sciences. Student-driven project office "the FIRMA" operates like a small company providing development projects to both university internal and external customers. Typical assignments include website designs, small-scale database applications, and end user training sessions. In addition, the FIRMA participates in several externally funded R&D projects, such as "Hot Potato". Students in the FIRMA learning environment gain relevant interdisciplinary skills by participating in many customer and R&D projects. Multicultural teams do innovative work together to meet the goals of the customers. For every project, a student project manager is chosen who is responsible for scheduling and coordinating the project. In agile projects, student project manager is Scrum Master. Depending on the project, teacher or customer is Product owner and responsible for communicating the needs of the customer for the project team. This approach not only deepens the disciplinary, but also interdisciplinary knowledge. Thus, project management skills are trained in authentic context.

KEYWORDS : SCRUM, Agile project management, R&D learning environment, ICT, Project-based learning

2.

Transforming Public Procurement Contracts Into Smart Contracts

Dr Pauline Debono BA Mag Juris LL.D

Abstract

The terms governing the provision of supplies, services or works by an economic operator to a governmental entity are set into a public contract that is signed following a procurement process. This paper explores whether government can utilise smart contract to incorporate the terms governing the provision of supplies, services or works. The fundamental elements of a contract are assessed in order to determine whether a smart contract can be considered as fulfilling these requirements. Following this assessment, the main hurdles to the use of smart contracting are examined and a possible solution proposed. The case for utilising smart contracting within the realm of public procurement is finally advocated.

Keywords: Public procurement, Elements of Contract, Smart Contracts

3.

Improving a Smartphone's Power Consumption - Application for an Automated Travel Diary

Michael Camilleri, Adrian Muscat, Victor Buttigieg and Maria Attard University of Malta
M. Camilleri, Department of Communications & Computer Engineering, Faculty of ICT, University of Malta;
A. Muscat, Department of Communications & Computer Engineering, Faculty of ICT, University of Malta;
V. Buttigieg, Department of Communications & Computer Engineering, Faculty of ICT, University of Malta;
M. Attard, Institute for Climate Change & Sustainable Development, University of Malta; M. Camilleri is now at School of Informatics, University of Edinburgh

Abstract

The ubiquity of smartphone devices and the availability of a variety of sensors have opened new opportunities for low cost, more detailed and more accurate spatial-temporal data collection. Nowhere is this more relevant than in the mobility and travel behaviour, where up till very recently the main form of data collection was through manually populated travel diaries. The successful use of electronic data collection methods through smartphones depends on a (i) ease of use perceived in terms of user intervention frequency and (ii) the impact on battery consumption due to the continuous running of the data collection application. This paper reviews existing methodologies for battery-aware location tracking and trip registration. The focus is on the specific need of energy-saving in an automated travel diary application for smart phones, which collects travel behaviour from volunteers. The automated travel diary is designed to make the data collection process as seamless to the user as possible. Within this context a battery-saving scheme is proposed and implemented on an Android system. The algorithm is tested on the field and the tests are conducted on various devices. The algorithm results in 50-70% savings in battery usage with little cost to data accuracy. The savings are enough to guarantee that the travel diary can be used through a whole day without re-charging, thus sustaining volunteer uptake. Keywords: Location-Tracking; Automated Travel Diary; Battery Awareness;

4

The Different Facets of Product Placement

Ivan De Battista
University of Wales

Abstract

Product placement is the intentional embedding of a commercial content into popular entertainment programmes with the sole purpose of encouraging purchase and ultimately consumption of the product.While traditional advertisingis reducing in popularity due to the zipping and zapping choices in the new television/online era, product placement is more strategically promising, popular and effective in films and television series. It is becoming more common a marketing tool for marketers to utilise in order to engage the audience and avoid the zapping phenomena.The product distinction and presentation of the advertisement has an interactive impact. This systematic literature review aims to give a broader understanding of the different aspects of product placement. In fact, related extracts from books, and articles appearing in the international journals from late 80s up to 2014 are collected and investigated, to examine the different categories of product placement, to understand the evolution and effectiveness of this promotional method and on the other hand, to show the downside of using product placement.

Keywords:- product placement, visual placement, verbal placement, effectiveness, advertising

5.

Quality of Experience Models for Game on Demand in Cloud-Based Infrastructure

Audrey Zammit, Department of Communications and Computer Engineering, University of Malta.
Audrey Zammit is now at the Department of Geosciences, University of Malta.
Adrian Muscat, Department of Communications and Computer Engineering, University of Malta.
Saviour Zammit, Department of Communications and Computer Engineering, University of Malta.

Abstract

The gaming experience while playing a cloud-based game depends on various factors and predicting the gaming experience makes a useful tool for the game cloud service provider, in both understanding system performance and automation. A test bed, made up of two computers and a network emulator, was set up to model a gaming cloud. The set-up allows for the simulation of various different network conditions, and to capture and analyse the data being transferred between the client and the server. Nine factors that influence the gaming experience are identified. A test group of subjects were asked to play different games under different conditions and rate the experience using an adaptation of the Absolute Category Rating and the Degradation Category Rating defined by the ITU-T for evaluating video quality of multimedia applications. The data collected was used to train two models. The first is based on an Artificial Neural Network (ANN) and predicts the QoE as a Mean Opinion Score (MOS) based on the input factors. The second model is a Naive Bayes Classifier (NBC) that makes use of the parameters as input to predict which level of opinion score the gaming experience is most likely to fall into. Both models perform well when predicting the opinion score. The correlation between the predicted and the subjective opinion scores is 0.74 for the NBC and 0.66 for the ANN.

Keywords: quality of experience, machine learning, cloud gaming, modeling

8.

An Effective Cybersecurity Training Model to Support an Organizational Awareness Program: The Cybersecurity Awareness TRAining Model (CATRAM)

Regner Sabillon Internet Interdisciplinary Institute (IN3) Universitat Oberta de Catalunya (UOC) Barcelona, Spain regners@athabascau.ca
Victor Cavaller Information and Communication Sciences Universitat Oberta de Catalunya (UOC) Barcelona, Spain vcavaller@uoc.edu
Jordi Serra-Ruiz Internet Interdisciplinary Institute (IN3) Universitat Oberta de Catalunya (UOC) Barcelona, Spain jserrai@uoc.edu
Jeimy Cano School of Business Universidad del Rosario Bogota, Colombia jeimy.cano@urosario.edu.co

Abstract

Traditional cybersecurity, security or information security awareness programs have become ineffective to change people's behavior in recognizing, failing to block or reporting cyberthreats within their organizational environment. As a result, human errors and actions continue to demonstrate that we are the weakest links in cybersecurity. This article studies the most recent cybersecurity awareness programs and its attributes. Furthermore, we compiled recent awareness methodologies, frameworks and approaches. We introduce a suggested awareness training model to address existing deficiencies in awareness training. The Cybersecurity Awareness TRAining Model (CATRAM) has been designed to deliver training to different corporate audiences, each of these groups with specific content and separate objectives. We concluded our study, by addressing the need of future research to target new approaches to keep cybersecurity awareness focused on the everchanging cyberthreat landscape. CATRAM has been tested, implemented and validated along with the CyberSecurity Audit Model (CSAM) in a Canadian higher education institution. A research case study is being conducted to validate both models and the findings will be published accordingly.

Keywords—cybersecurity, cybersecurity awareness model, cybersecurity awareness

9.

System Models To Improve SNR for CI's external devices Wireless Communication

Prof.Ramesh K, Prof.Rohitha Ujjinimatad, Prof.S.B. Kulkarni Department of PG studies in Computer Science, Karnataka State Women's University, Vijayapur, India rvkkud@gmail.com, rameshk@kswu.ac.in Proudhadevaraya Institute of Technology,Hosapete,India rohitha_ujjini@rediffmail.com Department of Computer science SDM College of Engg &Tech, Dharwad,India sbkulkarni_in@yahoo.com

Abstract:

In our earlier two research papers we have proposed two'UART to WIFI modules' namely IEEE 802.15.4 and BLE 4.0 wireless architectures to establish wireless Communication Among Speech Processor and Transmitter 0f most recent cochlear Implant Naida CI Q90.The two proposed architectures are wireless communication systems which are much prone to adjacent noises hence quality of the voice gets degraded for the CI users.The signal to noise ratio (SNR) is one of the important measures for reducing the noise. Hence we have derived an mathematical expression in the energy detector model which is used to find the detection probability. This theoretical expression is evaluated under various values of Pfa and derived an expression to compute the predetermined threshold. The simulation shows the detection performance of energy detection over non fading AWGN channel in the noisy environment and results for great improvement in the detection performance with increase in SNR. We find good performance of the energy detector even at low SNR. Simulation results closely match with theoretical results. The proposed mathematical analysis in the model can be incorporated to sense the signal from the microphone in wireless CIs and shall be used in a clinical validation in a quiet environment.

Key Words: CI, SNR, ROC, AWGN, NRI Response, mapping.

10.

Using Big Data, Cloud Computing, and Analytics (BDCA) in Program Management1

Bongs Lainjo AFFILIATION: CYBERMATIC INTERNATIONAL

ABSTRACT

Introduction Integration of architectures that make use of big data analytics and cloud computing can help Information technology departments of both public and private agencies gain competitive advantage. This dynamic encourages innovations and leads to increased revenues. Actualization of cloud computing technologies provides a timely and cost-effective data management aimed at increasing the efficiency and effectiveness of the services. Such outcomes contribute to an increased security and agility. Setting The paper highlights the current global and regional trends of big data and cloud computing and analytics (BDCA). The regions include Africa, Asia, Europe, North and South America. The paper seeks to identify the impacts of using big data analytics and cloud computing by information technology departments of academic institutions, private and public agencies, and progress registered globally and by each region. Audience The target audience of the paper includes and not limited to academia, private and public organizations. Methodology various research articles covering the topic of big data, cloud computing and analytics were consulted during preparation and compilation of the paper. The relevant articles offered thetrend of big data analytics and cloud computing globally and in five regions of interest. There were different levels of how big data analytics and cloud computing has been embraced by both private and public agencies in their Information Technology departments. Attempts were also made to highlight developments in sampled thematic areas. However, limited access to appropriate data and relevant reports continue to be a major challenge. Findings. The research revealed the regional variations in the application of (BCA). North America and Europe registered a higher level of cloud computing services, at 363,804 and 240,780 petabytes in 2016 respectively. On the other hand; Africa, South America and Asia, apart from countries like Japan, were still struggling to achieve increased application of the new technology in managing and application of big data analytics. The successful application of big data analytics and cloud computing has not only revolutionized the information technology departments across the world, but also its impacts have been witnessed in almost every sector of the society. Thematic areas such as health, aviation, science and technology, research, education, manufacturing and finance have been among the main beneficiaries of this technological advancement. Also, people are effectively able to share information through social networks and stream live events from their remote areas. Conclusion The evidence shows the numerous benefits resulting from application of (BCA). The technology increased information sharing and promoted economic growth by optimizing the efficiency of services delivered in the society.

Keywords: Big Data, Cloud Computing, Data Analytics, Thematic Areas, Information Technology, Regions

13

Fuzzy Inference System for Efficient Lung Cancer Detection

G. R. Sinha[1], Rohit Raja[2], Raj Kumar Patra[3], [4]Lalit Garg
[1]Professor (ECE), Myanmar Institute of Information Technology Mandalay (Adjunct Professor of IIIT Bangalore)
[2]Professor (CSE), Sreyas Institute of Engineering and Technology Hyderabad, India
[3]Professor (CSE), CMR Technical Campus Hyderabad, India
[4]Professor, Faculty of Information and Communication Technology, University of Malta

Abstract
This paper suggests a lung cancer detection system with marked and unmarked nodules of cancerous elements are detected and classified. Lung cancer is said to be one of the leading cause of death and therefore, early identification of lung cancer can address the risk due to lung cancer. Computed tomography (CT) is used for lung cancer analysis and diagnosis, and manual process suffers with several challenges such as poor accuracy. There are numerous research contributions in this area but research attempt towards robustness is all time challenge. We have implemented a fuzzy inference system which includes four important stages as pre-processing, image segmentation, feature extraction and design of fuzzy inference rules. These rules are usedto identify the cancerous cells accurately.

Keywords: Lung nodule, Fuzzy Inference System, Image Segmentation

15.

Deep Learning based Analysis and Classification of Medical Images in Indian context: Review and Recommendation

1G. R. Sinha and 2Lait Garg 1 Professor (ECE) and Dean (IQAC), CMR Technical Campus Hyderabad, India 2 Professor, Faculty of Information and Communication Technology, University of Malta

Abstract
Automated medical image analysis and diagnosis has become common in all modern hospitals and diagnostic centres. Numerous research contributions could be found on computer-aided diagnosis system (CADs) based methods for detection of abnormalities in different modalities of medical images. Though, the current literature suggests that has been limited research in the medical image

processing using deep learning. We, in this paper have studied and reviewed few of prominent research papers both at national and international level. Critical review suggests that there is huge scope of deep learning based research on CAD and medical image analysis. We also have suggested an approach that can greatly help medical image processing related applications, especially in improving its accuracy.

Keywords: Deep learning; Convolutional neural network (CNN); Medical Images; Image segmentation, Machine Learning.

16

Classification of Brain Hemorrhages in MRI using Naïve Bayes- Probabilistic Kernel Approach

Nita Kakhandaki, Shrinivas Kulkarni, Ramesh K and Umakant Kulkarni

Abstract

Brain Hemorrhage is one type of stroke, which is caused due to artery burst in the brain, killing the brain cells because of bleeding. Therefore, to reduce the criticality among the patients, for treatment, the Doctors depend on accurate report on the location of hemorrhage. Magnetic Resonance Imaging (MRI) is one of the best imaging modality when functional and structural abnormalities are to be found. To aid the identification of presence of abnormality a novel NB-PKC algorithm for Effective Recognition of Brain Hemorrhages in MRI is proposed. A series of preprocessing is done, then the image undergoes Binary thresholding process for applying image mask on the hemorrhage region. Then for segmentation a Modified Multi-Level Segmenting Algorithm (MMLSA) is applied, using Minimal Local Binary Pattern and GLCM, combined features are extracted and finally for classification a novel Naïve Bayes- Probabilistic Kernel Classification is applied. These techniques designed could accurately identify the position and classified whether the image had an abnormality or not and could reduce human errors.

Keywords–Hemorrhage, Magnetic Resonance Imaging (MRI), Segmentation, Classification, Detection.

17

Deep Learning: E-commerce Time Series Forecasting

Houda Bakir and Hédi Zaher Datavora

Abstract

The purpose of this paper is to provide a forecasting univariate model to predict phone prices on European e-commerce shops using Long Short Term Memory neural network (LSTM) and Support Vector Regression (SVR). We propose a comparison study of time series forecasting models for these two techniques. The Long Short Term Memory, due to its architecture, is considered as a perfect solution to problems not solvable by classic Recurrent Neural Networks (RNN). On the other hand, the SVR model are very powerful machine learning method for both classification and regression. In fact, SVR model is able to predict the next day price with RMSE 28.098 Euros with univariate model.

Keywords— Time series forecasting, LSTM Neural Network, Support Vector Regression, e-commerce data, Machine Learning, Deep Learning.

18.

The Evolution and Dynamics of Electronic Health Record Systems (EHRSs)

Bongs Lainjo

Abstract:

The aim of this study is to review the transformation process involved in converting the current manual medical records (MMR) into electronic health record systems (EHRSs). The study also illustrates a life case study conducted by the author as stage one of implementation of the center for Medicare and Medicaid services (CMMS) electronic health record (EHR) incentive program (Cohen et al., 2015). The third objective is to thematically highlight the prevalence, achievements, challenges and prognosis of implementing EHRSs. The study is focused on global, regional and national geopolitical systems. A group of select industrial countries in North America, Oceanic, Asia, Europe and Scandinavia is used to illustrate the dynamics and transformation system of medical records from manual to electronic. The methodology that is used analyzes the global, regional and the national implementation rates of the electronic health records systems. The review is made based on the different governments' role in making sure that the system is a success without compromising the quality of service. Also physicians' attitudes towards the system were used as part of the review process. A comprehensive analysis of the whole EHRSs ecosystems is performed.

Keywords: EHRSs, Achievements, Prognosis, Prevalence, Evolution, Challenges, Dynamic, CMMS, Global, Regional, National, Gold Standard, Quality of Service.

23.

Measuring e-HRM effectiveness using CFA : a case of Indian IT Industry

Bhadoriya, M.C*., Patwardhan, M., Bajpai, N.
ABV-IIITM, Gwalior(M.P.), India

Abstract

Managing human resource is an extremely important and cumbersome process for any organization. The advancements in technology has helped mankind in human resource management (HRM) by the involvement of electronic media and the use of information technology (IT). This is termed as electronic Human Resource Management or e-HRM. This paper identifies the various factors of e-HRM to understand the concept in depth by measuring the e-HRM effectiveness through these factors. This paper uses the exploratory factor analysis (EFA) to identify the factors and confirmatory factor analysis to test the model fit for the conceptual model developed. The findings would be important for software companies in assisting them to understand and analyze factors which will lead to the effective e-HRM implementation. This study is important as to the best of the authors' knowledge, not much study has been done in India in this field. Also, the results would be able to act as a basis for other studies to understand the impact of e-HRM on IT industry

Keywords: e-HRM, Indian IT industry, e-HRM effectiveness, CFA

25

CORPORATE SOCIAL RESPONSIBILITY APPLICATION IN THE HEALTHCARE SECTOR: A BIBLIOMETRIC ANALYSIS AND SYNTHESIS

Gianpaolo Tomaselli, LalitGarg, VipulGupta , Peter Xuereb, Sandra C. Buttigieg

[1] *University of Malta, Msida MSD 2080 (Malta)*

[2] *Thapar University, Patiala, Punjab 147004 (India)*

Abstract

This paper reviews the literature to understand the current state of Corporate Social Responsibility (CSR) application and communication in the healthcare sector. First we provide a bibliometric analysis that quantifies the number of scientific publications regarding CSR in healthcare of the last ten years (2007-2016). Then, we present the theoretical framework. Starting from a brief summary of CSR literature, we explain peculiarities of the healthcare sector and contextualize the CSR debate in the healthcare context, identifying its current application and gaps. We review not only the application of CSR in healthcare but also analyze the topic of CSR communication, as well as the tools adopted by healthcare organizations to communicate their CSR activities in this sector.

Keywords— Corporate social responsibility (CSR); healthcare systems; healthcare communication; communication tools; literature review.

26

Fuzzy Semantic Networks: A Framework for Knowledge Representation

Atta-ur-Rahman, CCSIT, Department of Computer Science, Imam Abdulrahman Bin Faisal University, , PO Box 1982, Dammam, KSA
Gohar Zaman, Department of Computer Science, Faculty of Basic and Applied Sciences, International Islamic University, Islamabad, Pakistan
Nahier Aldhafferi, Abdullah Alqahtani, CCSIT, Department of Computer Information System, Imam Abdulrahman Bin Faisal University, PO Box 1982, Dammam, KSA

ABSTRACT
Knowledge Representation (KR) is one of the hottest areas of research in data mining, AI and big data analytics. Knowledge represented in an effective way, helps in easy traversal, searching, reasoning and inferencing. In this regard, several algorithms, techniques and methods has been proposed in the literature and implemented with their own pros and cons. Semantic Networks provide the means of KR. Though the concept of Semantic Networks is not new and it has been widely used, however, there exist certain limitations in it. To overcome these limitations a modified version is proposed in this paper that is named as Fuzzy Semantic Networks (FSN) in which the relationship between two concepts can be provided more realistically by means of fuzzy membership function instead of just an 'is a' link. In this way, a true relationship between any pair of entities can be represented. Moreover, as better representation promises a better retrieval, in this paper, it is projected that this concept can play a vital role in numerous applications. Certain application areas are highlighted where FSN can be used and the working order and algorithm structures with example are also presented.

Keywords
Knowledge Representation, Semantic Networks, Fuzzy Semantic Network, Information Retrieval

27

Proposing a Unified Software Metrics Suite

Yusuf U. Mshelia[1]*, Edoghogho Olaye[2], Simon T. Apeh[3]
[2,3]*Department of Computer Engineering,Faculty of Engineering, University of Benin,Benin-City, Nigeria.*

Abstract
Literature and the web have revealed proliferation in the fabrication of new software metrics (SM) and their automated representations. Count of software metrics have been on high increase with relatively unmonitored standardization in formalized documentation, validation and verification of metrics definitions. This has produced inconsistent user-defined metrics on the different tools that implement software metrics. The consequent draw-back in inconsistent metrics result is the foundation to trailing down standard and/or universal definition and interpretation of metrics output. This is necessary because inadequate standardization lead to situations where metric results generated by metric tools for a given metric differ hence interpreted wrongly. There is therefore need for the establishment and/or reinforcement of standards that monitor and track metrics evolution towards achieving homogeneity in metrics definitions and the tools that implement them. From reviews of literature, this paper is initiating a flexible implementation of new metrics model that unifies definition, interpretation, archiving, automation and consequently, extensibility. These rippling chained processes form the process model for a unified software metrics suite.

Keywords— software metrics, unified metrics suite, process model

28.

Machine Learning Techniques for the Determination and Prediction of Online Gambling Addiction

David Farrugia, Dr Lalit
Department of Information and Technology, University of Malta

Abstract

This review paper aims to analyse various machine learning algorithms and predictive analysis techniques with the scope to accurately predict online gambling addiction. Results gathered from several pieces of literature are observed in principle of possible limitations and strengths that each approach may entail. In conclusion, methods like Neural Nets and Random Forests prove to be two excellent approaches that should be researched further with regards to this field.

Keywords: machine learning, predictive analysis, gambling addiction, disordered gambling, supervised learning, unsupervised learning

29.

Entrepreneurial Competencies and Entrepreneurial Orientation: Moderating Effects of Firm Age and Firm Size

Weerakoon, C. , Lecturer, Uva Wellassa University of Sri Lanka
PhD Candidate, School of Management, RMIT University, Melbourne, Australia
Kodithuwakku, S.S. , Professor, Department of Agricultural Economics and Business Management
Faculty of Agriculture, University of Peradeniya, Sri Lanka

Abstract

This study argues that moderating effects of firm age and firm size extend significant insights into firm behavior although extant literature has overlooked the influences by treating them as control variables. A sample of 51 micro, small and medium business owner-managers from Badulla Divisional Secretariat of Sri Lanka was studied by conducting in-depth interviews. Moderated linear regression test was mainly employed for data analysis and supported by simple slope test analysis. This approach uncovers that moderating effect of firm age on entrepreneurial competencies and entrepreneurial orientation relationship is stronger for small new firms and large older firms. This study offers important implications to future researchers on modeling the relationship between entrepreneurial competencies and entrepreneurial orientation.

Key words: entrepreneurial orientation, entrepreneurial competencies, Sri Lanka, small businesses, firm age, firm size

30

Handwritten Digits Classification using Convolutional Neural Networks

Ruihua Guo[1], Kalpdrum Passi[1],Lalit Garg[2], Chakresh Kumar Jain[3]
[1]{rguo@laurentian.ca, kpassi@cs.laurentian}, [2]{lalit.garg@um.edu.mt}, [3]{ckj522@yahoo.com},
[1]Department of Mathematics and Computer Science, Laurentian University, Sudbury, Ontario, Canada
[2]Department of Computer Information Systems, University of Malta, Malta
[3]Department of Biotechnology, Jaypee Institute of Information Technology, Noida, India

Abstract

This paper analyses the performance of Convolutional Neural Networks (CNN) for the classification of handwritten digits. A classical CNN model LeNet-5 is constructed layer by layer and applied to handwritten digits classification. A famous handwritten digits' database, MNIST, is used to test the CNN model proposed in the paper which produces high accuracy. By analyzing and comparing the output of the test data from the CNN model at different stages, we demonstrate the reasons LeNet-5 contains certain number of layers. Meanwhile, by comparing the error rate between different deep learning models on handwritten digit recognition, the performance of CNN surpasses the traditional methods, which confirms the efficiency and usefulness of CNN for image classification.

Keywords: deep learning, Convolution Neural Networks, LeNet-5, handwritten digits, MNIST

31.

Using New Marketing Technologies for Promoting Traditional Food Products

Teodora-Mihaela TARCZA , *Department of Management-Marketing, Faculty of Economic Sciences, University of Oradea, Oradea, Romania*
Postal address: Romania, Bihor, Oradea, Universitatii Street 1, 410087
E-mail: ttarcza@uoradea.ro
Adela-Laura POPA , *Department of Management-Marketing, Faculty of Economic Sciences, University of Oradea, Oradea, Romania*
Postal address: Romania, Bihor, Oradea, Universitatii Street 1, 410087
E-mail: apopa@uoradea.ro

Abstract
This paper aims to identify the ways in which producers of Romanian traditional food promote and commercialize in the digital era. Romanian manufacturers of traditional products are hardworking people preoccupied with the quality of the products that they so dearly prepare, but who are struggling to keep up with the latest marketing trends and technologies regarding advertising and commerce. This research is part of an ampler project aimed at identifying and describing consumer behaviour of traditional products. It endeavoured to find common factors between consumer behaviour and the manner in which producers manage to fulfil consumer needs. Therefore, this study is qualitative in nature, based on personal interviews. The results of this research will be disseminated to the producers involved in the study, in hopes of implementing the findings in their businesses. Scholars interested in traditional food products (TFP) can use this study as a reference point concerning the marketing activity of Romanian producers. One finding that was particularly interesting is that although producers are reluctant to use new technologies in their activity, they are willing to learn or ask help from the young and skilled.

Keywords: marketing technologies, traditional food products, semi-structured interviews, SMEs, Romania

32.

Coverage and Performance of Cellular Networks in Addis Ababa

Asrat Mulatu Beyene, Wireless Communication Systems, Addis Ababa University, Ethiopia, ambnn2001@gmail.com
Jordi Casademont Serra, Universitat Politècnica de Catalunya, Barcelona, Spain, jordi.casademont@entel.upc.edu
Yalemzewd Negash Shiferaw, Dep't of Electrical and Computer Engineering, Addis Ababa University, Ethiopia, yalemzewdn@yahoo.com
Ashagrie Getnet Flattie, Ethio Telecom, Ethiopia, edenashagrie@gmail.com

Abstract.
Mobile device penetration rate is increasing alarmingly and their interactive features are being enhanced daily. Moreover, their prices are diminishing attracting more users to the already overburdened cellular infrastructure of urban areas. To devise cost effective and appropriate solutions studying the coverage and performance of deployed cellular networks has primary

significance. In this work-in-progress paper an attempt has been made to collect real world user traffic data using commercial-grade mobile devices of various capabilities for three months. Results show that Addis Ababa is well covered with 2G, 3G and 4G mobile cellular technologies. In the business districts of the city, a mobile user has at least 80% of 3G and better network availability. Though, the networks behave as expected for the majority of the performance indicators some specific downsides are observed triggering further investigations. Overall, many residential areas have less coverage and performance of cellular networks.

Keywords: *Urban Area; Mobile Networks; Performance Evaluation; Heterogeneous Networks.*

33

The Digital Era of Customer Relationship Management

Adela-Laura POPA, *Department of Management-Marketing, Faculty of Economic Sciences, University of Oradea, Oradea, Romania*
Postal address: Romania, Bihor, Oradea, Universitatii Street 1, 410087
E-mail: apopa@uoradea.ro
Teodora-Mihaela TARCZA, *Department of Management-Marketing, Faculty of Economic Sciences, University of Oradea, Oradea, Romania*
Postal address: Romania, Bihor, Oradea, Universitatii Street 1, 410087
E-mail: ttarcza@uoradea.ro
Naiana Nicoleta ȚARCĂ, *Department of Management-Marketing, Faculty of Economic Sciences, University of Oradea, Oradea, Romania*
Postal address: Romania, Bihor, Oradea, Universitatii Street 1, 410087
E-mail: ntarca@uoradea.ro

Abstract
Nowadays, all marketers are aware of the fact that information technology has a tremendous impact on the way companies are achieving the marketing objectives. As a result, a lot of interest has emerged for topics like marketing technology or digital marketing technology. The development of this sector is extraordinary, reflected by the amazing growth regarding the number of tools (Brinker, 2017), but also the categories of marketing activities they target. In this paper we intend to describe how the digital environment changes the way the marketing activities are approached and, also, to synthesize the categories of benefits the digital information technology brought into the marketing world, especially regarding the customer relationship management (CRM). For that, we tried to capture the perspectives of both practitioners and academic literature. Our goal is to connect the digital marketing tools with the objectives of CRM, in order to understand how a digital tool contributes to the achievement of a CRM objective. This paper is part of a larger project and we consider it as a preliminary stage for further research. We intend to continue to analyze how the organizations use the digital tools in their customer relationship management activities, and to find out to what extent are they aware of the potential offered by the Internet and the related digital technologies in developing data-driven customer-centric marketing strategies.

Keywords: marketing technology; digital marketing; customer relationship management; CRM; information technology; digital era.

35

Spatial and Temporal Analysis of Crime Hot Spots in GIS, A Case Study of Kerman City, Iran

Ahmad Pourahmad 1, Mohammad Ehsan Ebrahimi 2, Ali Hosseini 1 ?, Mohamad Molaei Qelichi 1,
1 Department of Geography, University of Tehran, Tehran, Iran
2 Department of Law and Criminology, University of Tehran, Tehran, Iran

Abstract.

Personal incentives and those features of environment that creates felony are both important in crime generation. However, analysing each of these is not simple at the same rate. In general, all abnormalities and all social atrocities against every society's values are referred to as crime. In any way that it is committed has a time and place basis. More importantly, the difference between place conditions and behaviour characteristics, besides the time factors, entail uneven spatial distribution of crime in geographical environments. This study tried to investigate the relationship between demographic and ecological factors with crime rate and also to identify crime hotspots in the city of Kerman. According to this, the current research, focusing on recognizing geographical analysis of drug crimes in Kerman city, shows that the main centre of drug crimes is in accordance with the central area around the city and it is tended from the centre of the city toward the east and west. Firozabad district as the first crime hotspot in Kerman with a number of 86 people per acre is higher than the average of population density in the whole city of 40 people per acre. This point indicates that there is a positive and significant relationship between population density and crime hotspots of drugs in this city.

Keywords: Criminality Space Analysis, Crime Geography, Population Density, Geographical Information System (GIS), Kerman City.

36

A Keystroke Dynamics Dataset and Smartphone App

Darren Cilia Frankie Inguanez, Institute of Information & Communication Technology
University College Malta College of Arts, Science and Technology, Corradino Hill, Paola, PLA 9032
fdarren.cilia.a100674, frankie.inguanezg@mcast.edu.mt

Abstract

Research in keystroke dynamics has been around since 1980, initially on mechanical keyboards, and has gradually evolved to virtual keyboards, most notably on smartphones. The main purpose is for reinforcing active modes of authentication, such as use of passwords and pin codes, yet is also used for continuous passive modes of authentication. One of the initial challenges faced by research in this area is finding an existing dataset, the absence of which leads to the development of an application to gather data. We have noticed that interest in this area is increasing, albeit recent technology such as Touch ID and Face ID having a high accuracy. After, researching this area, we are publishing our dataset and smart phone application for public use. Our most recent research led to an equal error rate of 0.44% when classifying the owner of a smart phone after typing a short sentence using one hand, and an overall equal error rate lower than 1% for other modes. We believe that our application offers enough flexibility for other researchers to focus their time and energy on proving different hypothesis.

37

Low Power BLE Module for Wireless Communication among Speech Processor and Headpiece (Transmitter) of Cochlear Implants

S. B. Kulkarni, Prof. Ramesh K, Department of Computer Science and Engineering, SDM College of Engg. & Tech., Dharwad, sbkulkarni_in@yahoo.com
Department of PG studies in Computer Science, Karnataka State Women's University, Vijayapur, India, rvkkud@gmail.com, rameshk@kswu.ac.in

Abstract
Recent cochlear Implants Naida CI Q70 and Q90 from Advanced Bionics have their external devices such as speech processor and head piece a transmitter, Communicate with the reliable connection oriented network architecture. This architecture is complex with a long cable connected between the speech processor and headpiece (transmitter). This type of structure has several drawbacks, like maintenance of cable, the repair cost is high. To overcome these problems, an idea is to Design Wireless Communication system for a CI device is the thought process. The proposed Architecture uses the 'UART to BLE 4.0 Wi-Fi module to configure Speech Processor and Head Piece (Transmitter) of CI as BLE 4.0 module that has a hotspot for communication. Simulation results are shown.

Key words: Cochlear Implant, IC, Sound Processor, Transmitter, head piece, Electrode, Sound wave, Wi-Fi.

38

The Applicability of Process-Orientation to Software Development Projects

Viktorija Ponomarenko, Faculty of Computer Science and Information Technology, Riga Technical University, Riga, Latvia, viktorija.ponomarenko@gmail.com

Abstract
The progress in the Digital Single Market (DSM) have been acknowledged as one of the 10 political priorities by the European Commission since 2015 [1]. It could contribute to € 415 billion per year (GDP) to the economy of the EU 28 Member States and create hundreds of thousands of new jobs. Nowadays, the ICT sector and the European Digital Agenda have declared also as one of the seven pillars of the Europe 2020 strategy [2]. In order to speed up the development of new information technology and its commercialisation, it is necessary to increase the income of research organisations and to develop a new technology transfer model aimed at accelerating and improving the technology transfer taking into account process quality management. The aim of this study is to give an overview to a new approach to producing an additional value of the software development projects to improve the technology transfer process.

Keywords: Process Assessment; Process-Orientation; Six Sigma; Software Quality Management; Software Engineering.

39.

Sub-task scheduling with sequence dependent switch-over time in cloud computing

Amit Kumar Bhardwaj1, Yuvraj Gajpal2, Vipul Gupta3
1,3L.M. Thapar School of Management, Thapar Institute of Engineering & Technology University, Dera Bassi Campus, Punjab (India)
2 Supply Chain Management, Asper School of Business, University of Manitoba, Canada

Abstract:
This paper presents task scheduling in cloud computing environment. Many parallel computing resources work simultaneously in cloud computing environment to process the jobs submitted by

the end users. Each job is divided in the number of sub-tasks which can be processed independently. When a resource start processing a new sub-task, it requires preparation time called switch-over time. A sequence dependent switch-over time arises between the executions of two sub-tasks. Each combination of sub-tasks processed consecutively requires different switch-over time. The objective is to minimize total completion time to process all the inter-dependent sub-tasks, which are to be executed at a particular time. In this paper, two heuristic and one met heuristic algorithms are proposed to solve the problem. An extensive numerical experiment is performed to assess the performance of proposed algorithms.

Keywords: Cloud computing; scheduling; heuristic; met heuristic; parallel machine scheduling

41

The spisTRX: Causally-Consistent Read Transactions

Carl Camilleri, Joseph G. Vella, Vitezslav Nezval
Computer Information Systems
University of Malta, Malta

Abstract

Data Consistency defines how usable a data set is, and different levels of data consistency have been proposed. Causal consistency is one of these, and is the strongest type of consistency that can be achieved when data is stored in multiple locations, and fault tolerance is desired. Thespis is a middleware that innovatively leverages the Actor model to implement causal consistency over a DBMS, whilst abstracting complexities for application developers behind a REST open-protocol interface. Following our evaluation of correctness, performance and scalability of Thespis, in this paper we illustrate how a business application can be guaranteed causal consistency, but still encounter Time-To-Check-Time-To-Use (TOCTOU) race conditions. We subsequently present the design of The spisTRX, which builds upon, and extends, the Thespis middleware in order to offer read-only transaction capabilities, allowing clients to read a causally-consistent version of multiple data entities. A correctness analysis finally illustrates how our design avoids TOCTOU race conditions.

Keywords: causal consistency, distributed databases, actor model, middleware,
Transactions

42

High Level Architectural Modelling for Representing the Extract, Transform and Load Process

Tony Spiteri Staines[1], Joseph G. Vella[2]
[1]Dept. of Computer Information Systems, University of Malta
[2]Dept. of Computer Information Systems, University of Malta

Abstract

This work in progress paper identifies the necessity for high level architectural modelling when designing Extract, Transform and Load (ETL) processes for updating Data Warehouses (DW). ETL processes have become quite complex when they operate over the prevalent heterogeneous systems and the myriad of deployed technologies. The focus of previous works has been mainly on process modelling at a low level ignoring the architectural specification. The many solutions given in literature, and presented here in the related works part, are tied to very specific scenarios. In this paper the problem definition is formulated and a basic practical solution for conceptually modelling an ETL process using UML class diagrams is given. The approach that is being presented here will allow designers of ETL processes to create top-down and bottom-up solutions that are more implementable in respect to the resources, technologies, and available data. This solution should simplify the architectural representation required to describe the data sources and the ETL processes. Various key problems that remain unresolved are mentioned and discussed.

Keywords: Architectural Modelling, Business Requirements, Software Engineering, Requirements Engineering, Data Warehousing, ETL Processing.

43

The impact of eHealth adoption on patient pre-consultation waiting time; a comparative assessment of two district hospitalsin Abuja Nigeria.

Dr. Iniobong EkongMBBS,MPH,*Cert., GMEIT (Cobit 5)*[1];Engr. Emeka Chukwu M.ISM *GMEIT (Cobit 5)*[2]; Dr. Mohammed B. Kawu MBBS,MHM[1]

Department of Health Planning Research and Statistics, FCT Health and Human Services Secretariat, Abuja, Nigeria[1.] Faculty of ICT, University of Malta[2]

Abstract:

Evidence to support widespread adoption of digital health tools in hospitals is still lacking, and proof of their acceptance within the health system is largely missing. This study compared patient's pre-consultation waiting time (Time interval between the payment point, registration point, nursing point and entry into the consulting room) in two FCT hospitals, one using paper based registration system and the other using an electronic (eHealth) registration system.

Structured questionnaires wereadministered to both patients and health workers to determine and compare factors affecting care delivery wait times and howthe use or non-use of eHealth in patient's registration process influence it.In addition, patient wait times were measured in both hospitals at three care points – pay point, registration point and nursing station.

Key words: Pre-consultation waiting time, eHealth, digital health, structured training program, electronic Hospital information system, Wuse District Hospital, Maitama District Hospital.

44.

COMMON PERCEIVED PREDICTORS OF JOB SATISFACTION AMONG FILIPINO STAFF AND EMPLOYEES IN HO CHI MINH CITY, VIETNAM

Perfecto G. Aquino, Jr., Duy Tan University, Danang City, Vietnam

Divya Prakash Shrivastava, Dubai Women's College Higher Colleges of Technology Dubai, United Arab Emirates

ABSTRACT

The main objective this paper is to find out the most common predictors of job satisfaction amongst Filipino staff and employees in two selected manufacturing firms and its subsidiaries in Ho Chi Minh City which have employed a big number of Filipinos. These selected companies in Vietnam have for the past 30 years preferred to hire Filipino workers due to the fact that previous staff and employees especially in the manufacturing sector have proven their mettle/worth in the management and stewardship of the companies together with their technical skills and know-how. The data required for the study was collected from the participants selected for the study on the basis of stratified random sampling. The sample size was 406 respondents both locally and foreign-owned companies in Vietnam. Data were collected using the Employee Satisfaction Questionnaire developed by the Human Resource Management of Nike Company Limited in Vietnam to gather data on the predictors of job satisfaction of staff . The instrument is purely an objective checklist made of words or phrases to emphasize how well the word and/or phrases describe their work on present job, management, recognition, opportunity, promotion and people on present job.

Key words: job satisfaction, job security, salary, predictors, reward, work motivation, job security and promotion

45

A Systematic Review on QoS aware Resource Utilisation and Allocation in Cloud Computing

Vijay Prakash1, Seema Bawa1, Lalit Garg2
1Thapar University Patiala, India
2University of Malta, Msida
vijaysoni200@gmail.com, seema@thapar.edu, lalit.garg@um.edu.mt

Abstract:
Cloud computing has become popular computing model as it provides various services through Internet on pay-per-use model. Resource management of this computing model is a critical part which involves identification, selection and allocation of the appropriate resource for the user's request. Cloud users request for a service to Cloud Service Providers (CSPs), use it according to their needs and pay for the services used. Due to increasing demand of cloud resources it is challenging to utilise and allocate resources properly. Various factors such as resource heterogeneity, unpredictable and variable nature of the workload and diversified objectives of the users make it very difficult to allocate the appropriate resources to the users according to their Quality of Service (QoS) based requests. It is also mandatory to satisfy the Service Level Agreement (SLA) between cloud providers and cloud users for resource allocation. In this paper, various resource utilisation and QoS based resource allocation schemes in cloud computing has been reviewed and a comparative analysis has been done based on various parameters.

Keywords: Quality of Service; Resource Utilisation; Resource Allocation; Resource Management.

46

Women Entrepreneurship Challenges: An Indian Perspective

Ena Chopra[1]Esha Chopra[2]
IIM Bangalore, India
[1]ena.chopra@iimb.ac.in, [2]esha.chopra@iimb.ac.in

Abstract
The paper aims to evaluate the challenges faced by women entrepreneurs in India (a developing country). The paper examines the holistic opportunities created by entrepreneurial ecosystems and its impact on women entrepreneurship in the country.
Research Methodology: The interpretive research methodology was adopted in this paper. The interviews conducted with ten nascent women entrepreneurs gave an opportunity to understand their perspective and individual challenges in establishing businesses in India.
Findings: The findings presented in this paper describe the importance of entrepreneurial ecosystem and its impact on women entrepreneurs in India. The paper draws an analysis of the challenges faced by women entrepreneurs and their experience as an entrepreneur in India. Originality: The originality of the paper lies in evaluating the services offered in an entrepreneurial ecosystem, challenges faced by women entrepreneurs in India that influence their propensity towards entrepreneurship.

Keywords: Women entrepreneurs, Entrepreneurial ecosystem, Entrepreneurship in India, Start-up India

47

Enhance PEGASIS Algorithm for increasing the Life Time of Wireless Sensor Networks

Dinesh Sharma*, Geetam Singh Tomar**
Department of Computer Science Engineering, Uttarakhand Technical University, Dehradun THDC, IHET Tehri

ABSTRACT
The paper introduce an enhanced power efficient gathering in sensor information systems protocol which is used in wireless sensor networks to reduce the energy of the sensor nodes and increase the life time of the WSNs. The main problem in WSNs is that these sensor nodes have a limited energy and also these are not rechargeable so the only solution is to reduce that energy by designing type of protocol which is based on energy efficient routing. So we have enhanced the pegasis protocol in which we deploy some sensor node in the geographical area and then we form some cluster based upon the sensor nodes and then these individual clusters are used to form the chain from the sensor node and, In this way we can reduce some energy and also we can reduce the delay problem in the PEGASIS protocol. We proposed E-PAGASIS multi hop routing algorithm, increasing the lifetime of network and reducing the energy loss. Proposed algorithm is more efficient from existing PEGASIS algorithm .All the experimental results done by MATLAB.

Keywords:-Wireless Sensor Network, PEGASIS, Routing Protocol,Multihop,Base Station

48

Multi-Dimensional Indexes in DBMS

Thomas Mercieca, Joseph G. Vella
Faculty of ICT, University of Malta, Malta

ABSTRACT
Higher-dimensional data is becoming a necessity across multimedia, data mining and other data-driven applications where improvement in performance is desired but resources are limited. The R-Tree is a well-known index structure which DBMSs are implementing as core functionality for efficient retrieval of multidimensional data. Searching an R-tree is a multipath problem and the gap between the best and worst-case performance is very wide for this reason. Thus, building a quality R-tree in a short amount of time is especially important; several R-Tree variations exist to address this characteristic. Many of these variations differ in how the structure is developed when node overflows manifest themselves during the building process. In this work, we investigate the specific technique that Post greSQL uses, as an advanced and mature open-source DBMS, for its R-tree implementation. We focus on a specific parameter related to node overflows as an optimisation target to a well-known workload, and then propose a set of optimal values for it. There are several other configurations which influence the R-Tree, however, we focus on a specific one to be able to minimise the influences that arise out of a combination of variables. This parameter is hard-wired into the Post greSQL DBMS, and therefore, the DBMS engine source code is unravelled to allow this parameter to become accessible through an SQL construct for definition by the access method designer. The access method designer can resort to configuring this parameter when trying to meet specific performance targets in terms of storage utilisation or query execution. Because of this project's implementation, access method designers now have a more flexible and configurable set-up of their multidimensional data indexes requirements.

Keywords: R-Tree, index node overflows, splitting heuristics, multidimensional indexes, PostgreSQL DBMS

50

A RESEARCH ON DETERMINING THE RELATIONSHIP BETWEEN COMPETITIVE STRATEGIES AND HUMAN RESOURCE MANAGEMENT PRACTICES

Yasemin BAL
Yildiz Technical University, Turkey

Abstract
The role of human resources has gained more importance in the last decades. Organizations have started to see their employees as a source of competitive advantage. Parallel to this perspective, strategic human resources management has become even more important. According to this view, organizations should link their competitive strategies with HR functions and practices of the organization. Each HR function should be aligned with the strategy of the organization. Competitive strategies require different employee skills and HR practices so all functions of HR should be developed according to the objectives of the organization and integrated with organizational strategies. In this way, it will be possible to follow the strategies effectively and improve the performance of the organization and employees. Organizations that can integrate their strategies with HR functions can perform better and gain competitive advantage. This study aims to explore the differences between organizations' HR practices in terms of their competitive strategies. The research is important in filling the gap in the related literature and also it provides guidance to organizations for gaining competitive advantage. The findings of the research from 63 companies in Fortune Turkey list are discussed.

Key Words: Competitive Advantage, Strategic Human Resources Management, Competitive Strategies, Differentiation, Cost Leadership.

51

An Artist's Expert System: second order cybernetics for matching users to bespoke books

Dr Eleanor Dare
Royal College of Art
School of Communication
eleanor.dare@rca.ac.uk

Abstract
All books should be intelligent, but how can books be produced which use computerised systems and analytical methods, processes more commonly deployed in business intelligence or medicine, to analyse readers and learn from them? This paper investigates the use of an Expert System for matching users to bespoke books. The work is positioned within the context of the author's role as a senior tutor at the Royal College of Art, School of Communication. The author's artistic practice is concerned with the interface of technology and storytelling, the work presented here is used as a case study, aiding students and researchers in understanding the limits and possibilities of Good Old Fashioned Artificial Intelligence and its presence within an art and design context, as well as outlining the process and intentions of developing an intelligent system for matching users to books.

Key words: Expert Systems, Artificial Intelligence, Machine Learning, Digital Humanities, Art and Design, Cybernetics

52.

Petrochemical Process Time-series Forecasting using Artificial Neural Network

Audu Eliazar Elisha1, Lalit Garg2, Akujobi-Emetuche Grace3
1,2Computer Information Systems, University of Malta.
3University of PortHarcourt

Abstract

Forecasting has always been part of industrial process operations, and is key to management planning. In this paper, we explore the potentials of machine learning to predict tank levels, which is the fundamental aspect of measurement and control in Oil and Gas industries. First, accurate tank level prediction model significantly optimised ullage (storage space) management and enhance timely planning of petroleum products movement in a value chain management. Secondly, the use of level prediction models can serve as a tool to monitor storage tank level sensors for faults and accuracy deviation. We used plant variables such as pump power consumption, specific gravity of the fluid and pump's discharge pressure to estimate a product tank level. Time series, nonlinear artificial neural network (ANN) technique has been adopted to extrapolate storage tank levels many hours in advance. Using data logged from pumping activities in Port-Harcourt Refinery and Pipeline and Product Marketing Company (PPMC), the neural network prediction model is tested and validated.

Keywords—Measurement and Instrumentation; Control loop; Artificial Neural Network; Particle Swarm Optimization; Sensors; Industrial Control.

53.

Survey of Breast Cancer Detection Using Machine Learning Techniques in Big Data

Madhuri Gupta and Bharat Gupta, (PhD Scholar and Assistant Professor)
madhurigupta26@gmail.com and bharat.gupta1@gmail.com
Department of Computer Science & Engineering, Jaypee Institute of Information Technology, Noida, India

Abstract

Cancer is chunk of disease in which cells in body grow and divide beyond the control. Breast cancer is second most common disease after lung cancer in women. Incredible advances in Health sciences and biotechnology have prompted a huge creation of information, such as high throughput gene expression and clinical data, created from massive Electronic Health Records (EHRs). To analyze this vital amount of data, data analytics and machine learning techniques are available to intelligently extract valuable information from available data. Major goal of this study is to discover the most precise techniques and tools for breast cancer detection. So, this paper study will focus on systematic review of the application of machine learning method, data analytic techniques, tools and frameworks in the field of breast cancer research with respect to a) Cancer survivability, b) Cancer recurrence and c) Cancer prediction and detection at primary stage. There are many machine learning techniques are employed in breast cancer research some are characterized as supervised learning others are unsupervised learning techniques. Support Vector Machine and Artificial Neural Network are found widely used techniques whereas Apache Spark found most compatible data processing engine with all machine learning frameworks.

Keywords: Breast Cancer, Machine Learning, Big Data Analytics

54

A Review of Cyber Security Risk Assessment across Financial Sector

Mr. Rahul Sharma, Lovely Professional University, School of Computer Applications, Phagwara, India
Dr. Rudra Rameshwar, Thapar Institute of Engineering & Technology (Deemed University), L.M. Thapar, School of Management, Patiala, India

ABSTRACT

Banking Sector and other financial institutions handle some of the most private or sensitive data from account profile and digital card data for personal identification. With the financial pulse of both individuals and organisations on the base line, cyber security for banking sector is more constitutive. Unfortunately, it is also under cyber attack more than ever before. The proposed paper aims to get an oversight of the cyber crime as it is defined and revealed by essential literature, historical outputs and international provision and perform an analysis of cyber-attacks reported globally over the years in order to compose the trends in digital-crime. Based on the proposed statistics, findings and surveys, we proposed software that is developed to protect individual Microsoft Windows personal data as well as Microsoft Windows Server private or financial corporate data. It is an initiate in order to improve digital security that would support to protect business as safeguard from hackers on private data security perspective.

KEYWORDS: Cyber Security, Cyber Attack, Cyber Crime, Digital Crime, KDD, UNM, RSA, Cryptography.

55

A Comparison of Touch-Screen Interface and Voice-User Interfaces: An Explorative Study for Multi-Modal Design

Daniel Edward Galea, University of Malta
Peter Xuereb, University of Malta

ABSTRACT

A graphical user interface in a mobile device does not accommodate all the different contextual scenarios that users might find themselves in. Furthermore, screen-size might also be an issue. This paper compares, through iterative usability testing, a graphical user interface and a voice user interface on a mobile device, so that their strengths and weaknesses on this type of device can be noted. Also, these user interfaces are combined to analyse the benefits or limitations brought on by multi-modal user interfaces. The results presented in this paper show how a multimodal user interface benefits the users, and also where and how the uni modal UIs perform better and how they can be used to mitigate each other's flaws

56

A Mathematical Model to Solve the TALBP with Tools Sharing by Parallel Workstations

Rupesh Nishad, Ramawatar Kulhary, Sunil Agrawal
Department of Mechanical Engineering, Indian Institute of Information Technology, Design and Manufacturing Jabalpur

Abstract:

A two-sided assembly line is a type of production line where tasks are performed in parallel at both sides of the line. The line isoften found in producing large size products such as trucks and buses. This paper develops a mathematical model for a two-sided assembly line balancing problem (TALBP) with tools sharing. Objective of the model is to minimize the cost of assembly line by sharing the costly tools between the parallel workstations. To check the efficiency of the proposed model, 22 well-known benchmarks set of problem are solved. The experimental results demonstrate that the proposed model is efficient. Solutions to these problems are obtained with the help of Lingo 16.0 by using the "global solver" option as the solving method to search the global optimum solutions. The mathematical model can be extended further by including suitable constraints for sharing workers between parallel workstations.

Keywords: Assembly Line Balancing, Two-sided Assembly Line Balancing, Tools sharing

57

Can ICT Enhance the Performance of Indian Agriculture Fresh Supply Chain?

RakeshPatidar[a], Sunil Agrawal[b] and B P Yadav[c]

[a,b]*Mechanical Engineering Discipline, PDPM Indian Institute of Information Technology, Design and Manufacturing, Jabalpur, India*

[c]*Indian Institute of Materials Management (National Counsellor), NHQ- Mumbai, India*

Abstract

Indian agriculture fresh supply chain (AFSC) is run by unorganised large number of intermediaries and there is no proper interaction between farmer and customer. These lead to over/under production and high wastages of produces thereby, results in low profit to the farmer. According to literature review, information communication and technology (ICT) can be a major tool to improve the efficiency and effectiveness of a supply chain (SC). The purpose of this paper is to explore the possibilities to use ICT for enhancing the performance of Indian AFSC. Authors identify strengths, weaknesses, opportunities and threats (SWOTs) of existing Indian AFSC through literature survey. The focus is to develop the suitable ICT strategies for overcoming internal weaknesses as well as external threats with the help of internal strengths and external opportunities by exploring the feasible combinations between the two. Twenty ICT strategies are developed which are further deduced according to their belongingness into four types. These strategies fall under the four major AFSC activities such as agriculture production, logistics, business actions and demand supply integration. Hence, the developed strategies will help researchers and policy makers in modelling/redesigning Indian AFSC to enhance the performance of the chain.

Keywords- Agriculture fresh supply chain (AFSC); Information communication and technology (ICT); Strategy formulation

58

A NEW PARADIGM WITH NEW CHALLENGES FOR DIGITAL FORENSICS - A FRAMEWORK FOR PERFORMING DIGITAL FORENSIC INVESTIGATIONS ON CLOUD-BASED SYSTEMS

Alex Williams1

Lalit Garg2

1 MSc IT Graduate, University of Liverpool, UK

2 Faculty of Information and Communication Technologies, University of Malta, Valletta, Malta

ABSTRACT

Cloud computing as we now know has created a paradigm shift from the traditional approach to computing. The adoption rate is increasing with benefits such as low cost and efficient use of resources. However, these benefits are accompanied by some challenges for computer forensics practice. The complexities of the cloud - its core characteristics and implementation all pose several challenges for computer forensic investigators. An impact assessment survey (survey 1) was conducted to determine the nature and extent of the impact. A total of 104 responses were gathered. The proposed framework consists of a set of guidelines and a model for cloud-based forensics. The framework was evaluated through an online-based evaluation survey (survey 2) that targeted 20 cloud computing and/or computer forensics professionals. The result from survey 1 confirms the impact of cloud computing on computer forensics, with a further indication that cloud inherent characteristics and design such as distributed storage, multi-tenancy and virtualization have posed varied challenges for the digital forensics process. Furthermore, the result concludes that the proposed framework addresses many of the issues and challenges under discussion with some degree of effectiveness and efficiency.

Keywords: Cloud computing, Computer Forensics, Cloud-based Forensics, Digital Evidence; Digital Forensic Investigation Process

62

Examining the impacts of information and communication technology (ICT) on academic research and information sourcing in Nigeria Universities

Fidelis Egoeze Late, Sanjay Misra, Adewole Adewumi, Robertas Damasevicius, Rytis Maskeliunas and Dr.Ravin Ahuja

Abstract

Information and communication technology (ICT) has changed the way academic research and sourcing of information are perceived and approached in higher education institutions. This study based on descriptive survey design investigates the impacts of ICT on research and information sourcing in Nigeria Universities. The study employed questionnaire as the research instrument, with the questionnaire items generated through review of related literature. A total of 192 respondents made up of students, lecturers, and administrators randomly selected from a total of nine universities in the North-central and South-East zones of Nigeria participated. Data collected were analysed using mean statistical analysis, Chi-square test of independence, and analysis of variance (ANOVA) at 0.05level of significance. The study identified major impacts of ICT on research and information sourcing in Nigeria Universities. Some suggestions were made for Nigeria universities to optimize the benefits of ICT in this area of application.

Keywords: ICT, research, information sourcing, Nigeria universities.

63

Classification and Prediction of Child Mortality Rate using Learning Algorithms

Nureni Ayofe Azeez, Oluwadamilola Tugbobo, Robertas Damasevicius, Sanjay Misra, Rytis Maskeliunas and Adewole Adewumi

Abstract.

About 2,300 under-five children are lost daily in Nigeria, making it the country with the world's second highest under-five child mortality (UFCM) rate. UFCM refers to the odds per 1,000 that a neonate will die before the age of five. There is therefore a great need to reduce child mortality, and improve child health in developing countries. Child mortality is a core indicator for child health and well-being. The mining of data is becoming increasingly popular, especially in healthcare because there is a need to conduct in-depth examination, and analysis of health data for identification of patterns, and detection of valuable information. The aim is to present new findings on child mortality using two popular learning algorithms, and to make comparison between the two methods. The research used Logistic Regression, and Naive Bayes classifier to predict trends and behavioural patterns from the under-five child mortality data set provided by the Institute for Health Metrics and Evaluation (IHME). It also analysed and investigated the predictors of child (aged 0 - 4 years) mortality rates in all the six geo-political zones in Nigeria.

Keywords: Child Mortality, Data Mining, Logistic Regression, Naive Bayes, Nigeria

64

A Markov Decision Process (MDP) Model for Pipeline Inspection with Unmanned Ground

Chika O.Yinka- Banjo, Mary I. Akinyemi, Charity O. Nwadike, Sanjay Misra, Adewole Adewumi and Robertas Damasevicius

Abstract.

Frequent inspection and proactive monitoring is crucial in monitoring the health of a pipeline else, leakages because of inner corrosion, pipeline wear out or vandalism of pipeline may lead to loss of lives and properties. This research addresses the challenges or limitations of pipeline inspection methods. We demonstrated how a simulation of pipeline inspection can be managed by Markov decision process (MDP). The proposed policy selection was controlled by an algorithm that manages how the mobile agent (unmanned ground vehicle) responds to observed conditions of the pipes in its immediate vicinity. Based on various simulated experiments the ground vehicle correctly detects defects in pipes without false alarm and stores details for the maintenance team to carry out necessary actions. The size of pipeline corrosion was measured by two different robots. Statistical tests were hence conducted to compare the performance of the 2 robots. The result show that variation in the size of corrosion for both robots is not statistically difference.

Keywords — Associated Probability, Associated Reward, Associated cost, Unmanned Ground Vehicles, Virtual Robot Experimentation Platform, Markov decision process.

65

MANAGEMENT OF ELECTRIC POWER IN NIGERIA

Johnson Ajiboye, Mary Ajiboye, Sanjay Misra, Victor Matthews and Dr.Ravin Ahuja

ABSTRACT

Currently, Nigeria has an installed electricity generation capacity for supply to the national grid of 12,522MW, with available capacity of only approximately 4,500 MW which even dropped to as low as 1,200 MW at a time, to meet the needs of Nigeria's population of more than 170 million and a country with a GDP growth rate of 7%. The Management of the Power Sector has been a great challenge. This research was carried out in Abuja Electricity Distribution Company (AEDC), Niger Region. AEDC is a major stake holder in the Power Sector. The study population for this research covers a Business Units of the Niger Region. Analysis of the data collected revealed that energy losses incurred the area office in 2016 is 46.33%, collection losses 62.50%, metering gap is 45% unmetered and customer to employee ratio is 863:1.

Keywords: Electricity, Management, energy losses, electrical power

66

Why e-Government Systems Fail: The Systems for the Labor Market

Fugini M.G.(1), Maggiolini P.C., and Salvador Valles, R.

Abstract

The difficulties in the development and implementation of e-government complex systems, such as those for the labor market, create worries for the responsible of Public Administrations (PA). In general, seldom are the results of analyses reported about the percentage of information systems that were unsuccessfully deployed. However, the analysis of failures is a recurring theme, which deserves special attention. The paper discusses some reasons of failure, considering the great social importance of information systems in PA and the high number of involved resources. We make a literature overview and identify some of the main causes of failure, based on analysis of e-government systems for the labor market for the case of BLL (Italy) and of SOC (Spain).

67

Cintent Marketing: An Action Research Approach to Developing a Customer Online Engagement Strategy

Cynthia D. Wiggins, Lalit Garg
University of Liverpool

Abstract

Within the last 12 years there has been a proliferation of companies and applications whose main products and/or services have been focused on the provision of individual and company generated content, and the engagement of customers including Buzz Feed, YouTube, Facebook, Twitter and Pinterest. Most organizations would admit that in the online arena the main success of their company lies in their ability to not only have customers view content about their organization but to identify, retain, sustain and engage current and potential customers; thereby implying that the strategy of content marketing must go beyond the mere provision of viral content and move more towards the development of an entire customer online engagement strategy/model. However, because most content and customer engagement strategies are developed by private companies, whose competitive advantage lies in their proprietary models, there have been few instances within the academic arena to fully investigate the antecedence and consequences of customer engagement within the context of content marketing.

Keywords: Content Marketing, Customer Online Engagement, Viral Marketing, Action Research

68

Artificial Intelligence, MOOC's and the Dilemma of Teaching and Learning in Tertiary Institutions: A Critical Appraisal

I. A. P. Wogu1, S. Misra2, P. A. Assibong3, H. A. Apeh4, E. Awogu-Maduagwu5
1, 3. Department of Political Science & International Relations, College of Leadership Development Studies, Covenant University, Ota, Ogun State, Nigeria.
2. Department of Electrical and Information Engineering, College of Engineering, Covenant University, Ota Ogun State, Nigeria.
4. Department of Counselling and Educational Psychology, Faculty of Education, University of Abuja Gwagwalada, Abuja, Nigeria.
5. Department of Languages and General Studies Program. College of Development Studies,

Abstract

Recent research on the application of Artificial Intelligence (AI) technology in the education industry for teaching and learning has stirred up a revolution via the use of platforms like the 'Massive Open Online Courses' (MOOC), the likes the world have never seen before. Millions through this platform can now enroll online to get one form of education or the other. Many scholars however doubt the quality of education transmitted and acquired via these platforms, hence, some scholars describe the education gotten through this medium as *artificial education*. A situation that has resulted to a kind of revolution in the education industry described as *Education Tsunami*. The Marxian theory of Alienation offers an appropriate theoretical platform for the analysis conducted in the paper. The Ex-post factor method of analysis and Deidra's critical analytic method was adopted for attaining the objectives of the paper. The dilemmas eroding the quality of education were identified. Blended learning approaches, as against present methods were recommended.

Keywords: Artificial Intelligence, Artificial Education, Alienation Theory Education Tsunami, Education Industry, MOOC's

69

Performance Comparision of Various Cryptographic Algorithms Along with Energy Consumption in Wireless Sensor Network

Bharat Mishra, Geetam Singh Tomar and Vivek Parashar

Abstract

Advancement in technology has given a huge opportunity in the field of sensors and sensor based technology, WSN of sensor nodes (SNs) in the network is the structure which is usually small in size and has low battery to communicate with other nodes. It contains memory and processors for sensing the data from the surroundings. In WSN sensor nodes are diffuse close to each other which may result into higher communication leads to failure of nodes. They can overcome node failure through easy exploiting other routing path. Routing is much complicated in this form of network as compared to other wireless networks and there are different routing protocols used to deploy the communication among the nodes. Energy consumption is one of the major issues in WSN to maintain the lifetime of the network. Entire network life span is depending on proficient energy exploitation in sensor network. In this paper, the challenges, limitations and characteristics of WSN has been discussed. There are various cryptographic algorithms available to improve the security of the network by the detailed analysis of the algorithms, the encryption and decryption of the different algorithms have been taken into consideration. The transmission can be performed to place the nodes in the network and provide the connectivity among the nodes securely.

Keywords—WSN, Routing, Energy, Security, Cryptographic Algorithms, RSA, AES, DES, NTRU, etc.

70

DEVELOPMENT OF A DECISION SUPPORT SYSTEM FOR IMPLEMENTING SECURITY STRATEGIES FOR DATA PROTECTION AND REGULATORY COMPLIANCE IN A CLOUD BASED HEALTH-CARE ENVIRONMENT

Amit Kumar Bhardwaj1, Lalit Garg2, Solomon Olalekan Oyenuga3, Divya Prakash Shrivastava4 1L.M. Thapar School of Management, Thapar Institute of Engg. & Tech., Derabassi, Punjab (India) 2Information & Communication Technology Department, University of Malta, Malta 3University of Liverpool, UK, 4Higher Colleges of Technology, Dubai, UAE

Abstract

Cloud computing has emerged as a fast growing system in the Information Technology world. Cloud computing is an infrastructural system that would greatly pave way for cost minimization, easier data accessibility, fast processing of information and the scalability feature which are the peculiar attractions it can provide. Cloud computing is increasing its scope to the different sectors where sensitive data are being handled. The trend will be a technology that will have an enhanced provision of security and a robust authentication which will be used to protect sensitive information or data. The Health-care industry is facing with lack of data integrity, lack of confidentiality of data and large cost of operations. Thus, there is the need to deploy an infrastructure that could be used to reduce the time consuming efforts of the health workers and the cost of running its operations. Hence, the need to adopt the infrastructure in order to have the Electronic Medical Records (EMRs) transferred to the Cloud where patients can easily have access to their records irrespective of the geographical location through the development of a Decision Support System (DSS). The purpose of this research is to develop a Decision Support System through the deployment of an in-house private Cloud based Architectural System. The study will explore the benefits, the limitation, and the barriers that could be faced when implementing a Decision Support System in a Healthcare Organization with the provision of a future reference. The adoption of the technology will help reduce the cost, help provide better interoperability with other Healthcare providers and the provision of an efficient management system in the Healthcare Industry.

Keywords: Cloud Computing, Decision Support System (DSS), Electronic Medical, Records (EMR), Health-Care Industry and the Cloud.

71

INVESTIGATION INTO CLOUD COMPUTING ADOPTION WITHIN THE HEDGE FUND INDUSTRY

Amit Kumar Bhardwaj1, Lalit Garg2, Thomas Cole3, Divya Prakash Shrivastava4 1L.M. Thapar School of Management, Thapar University, Derabassi, Punjab (India) 2 Information & Communication Technology Department, University of Malta, Malta 3 The University of Liverpool, UK, 4Higher Colleges of Technology, Dubai, UAE

Abstract

Cloud computing is a paradigm shift in how technology services are being delivered but differing cloud computing models bring varying benefits and risks. Cloud computing is not associated with a specific technology, instead it as an alternative method to deliver technology as a service. The United States and United Kingdom hedge fund industry was the focus sector for this paper. The paper investigates current cloud computing adoption, recognises catalysts for rejection or adoption and discusses the improvements to enhance cloud computing endorsement. Hedge fund technologists, prime service consultants, technology service providers, industry application vendors, investors and an independent information security consultant participated were surveyed for this paper. In summary, the paper acknowledges the growth of cloud computing in the hedge fund sector. Private cloud deployments are the strongly favoured model. The author highlights that the private cloud definition is vague and requires further classification, elaborating on the variants of private cloud. This is important as the variants of private cloud computing offer varying benefits and risk which the hedge fund sector has proven to be sensitive to. Equally, this paper argues that some of the current security concerns are over-stated and perhaps reflect a conservative decision making framework rather than a realistic consideration of the options.

Keywords: Cloud Computing, Hedge Fund, Decision Making

74

EXPLORING MOBILE CROWDSOURCING IN THE PUBLIC ADMINISTRATION

1Vasileios Yfantis, 2Peter Xuereb and 3Lalit Garg
1 Luleå University of Technology,
2,3University of Malta, University of Malta

Abstract

Crowdsourcing has been extensively used in the private sector and recently adopted by the public sector. The current paper discusses the use of the mobile crowdsourcing in the public administration from an IS perspective by exploring its current use and research challenges. The authors classify the mobile crowdsourcing in four categories, based on the application areas: Infrastructure maintenance, environmental reporting, critical situation reporting, crime watch reporting. Each application area is examined for its research challenges and the contribution of the authors in the crowdsourcing research area.

Keywords: Mobile devices, Crowdsourcing, Public administration.

75

A Review on Intrusion Detection Systems

Sharda Patel and Mamta Lambert

ABSTRACT

A Mobile Ad Hoc Network (MANET) is a collection of mobile nodes (hosts) which interact with each other via wireless links either directly or relying on other nodes as routers. MANET does not need a fixed network infrastructure; every single node works as both a sender and a receiver. Nodes interact directly with each other when they are both within the same communication range. Otherwise, they depend on their neighbors to exchange messages. The self-configuring ability of nodes in MANET has made it popular among critical objective applications like military use or emergency recovery. The nodes in MANET are resource constrained and vulnerable to various kinds of attacks such as gray hole, black hole, modification or Sybil attack, wormhole attack, and byzantine attack. Many intrusion detection systems came into existence to safeguard MANET from these attacks. The purpose of this paper is to reviews various existing techniques of IDS (intrusion detection systems) for MANET.

Keywords- MANET, IDS (intrusion detection system), Acknowledgement

76

Artificial Intelligence, Smart Class Rooms and Online Education in the 21st Century: Implications for Human Development.

Ikedianchi Ayodele Wogu1, Sanjay Misra2, Patrick Agbor Assibong3, Hosea Abalaka Apeh4, Esther Fadeke Olu-Owolabi5, Edith Abisola Awogu-Maduagwu6,

1, 3, 5. Department of Political Science & International Relations, College of Leadership Development Studies, Covenant University, Ota, Ogun State, Nigeria.

2. Department of Electrical and Information Engineering, College of Engineering, Covenant University, Ota Ogun State, Nigeria.

4. Department of Counselling and Educational Psychology, Faculty of Education, University of Abuja Gwagwalada, Abuja, Nigeria.

6. Department of Languages and General Studies Program. College of Development Studies, Covenant University, Ota. Ogun State, Nigeria.

Abstract

While the advent of Artificial Intelligence (AI) technologies in the education sector has largely taken over conventional class rooms and revolutionize the way education is conducted in the 21st century to the admiration of many, there are scholars who believe it is too early to celebrate the benefits of AI in the education sector, since modern AI teaching systems now raises long-term issues about the place of the teacher in AI education. The Marxist Alienation theory was considered for this paper. The Ex-post factor method of analysis and Deidra's critical analytic method was utilized for attaining the objectives of the paper. The paper faults recent attempts at eulogizing the impact of AI in the education sector and on human development. Extensive research is proposed as necessary for contemporary scholars in the field of AI and education technology before proper appropriation is made of its gains in education and human development.

Keywords: Artificial Intelligence, Alienation Theory, Education Sector, Human Development, Technological Devices, Smart Class Rooms.

78

Artificial Neural Network Model for Path Loss Predictions in the VHF Band

Segun I. Popoola[1,*], Nasir Faruk[2], Nazmat T. Surajudeen-Bakinde[3], Aderemi A. Atayero[1], Sanjay Misra[1]

[1] Department of Electrical and Information Engineering, Covenant University, Ota, Nigeria.

[2] Department of Telecommunication Science, University of Ilorin, Ilorin, Nigeria.

[3] Department of Electrical and Electronics Engineering, University of Ilorin, Ilorin, Nigeria.

Abstract

Artificial Neural Networks (ANNs) have been recently exploited to develop suitable models for path loss predictions. However, the ANN algorithm that provides the best results has not been well established neither has the models been characterized to limit their performances and applications in the various frequency bands. In this paper, we characterize the propagation path loss in the Very High Frequency Band (VHF) using different ANN learning algorithms and activation functions based on the measurement data collected at 203.25 MHz in an urban environment (Ilorin, Nigeria). The prediction results of Hata, COST 231, ECC-33, and Egli models at varying distances were fed into a feed-forward neural network and mapped to each corresponding measured path loss value. Statistical analysis shows that the ANN model that was trained with hyperbolic tangent activation function (HTAF), Levenberg-Marquardt (LM) algorithm, and 80 neurons in the hidden layer produced the most satisfactory results with Mean Error (ME), Root Mean Square Error (RMSE), Standard Deviation (SD), and coefficient of determination (R^2) values of 3.75 dB, 5.10 dB, 3.46 dB, and 0.95. However, the HTAF with Scale Conjugate Gradient (SCG) is more stable even though its prediction errors were slightly higher than that of LM.

Keywords: path loss prediction, radio propagation, ANN, activation function, learning algorithm.

AUTHOR INDEX

AUTHOR INDEX

International Association of Academicians Connecting Scholars, Scientists and Engineers (IAASSE)
www.iaasse.org
info@iaasse.org

CURRAN ASSOCIATES INC.
proceedings.com

ISBN 978-1-5108-5880-0
9 781510 858800

World Conference on Carbon (CARBON 2018)

Bonded by Carbon

Madrid, Spain
1-6 July 2018